Quick Cash Playbook

## ABOUT THE AUTHOR

Hi there! I'm just like you—a regular Jane trying to make life a little more manageable and my bank account a little less terrifying. I'm currently a medical student working my way toward becoming a doctor (not there yet, but one day!). Along the way, I've learned that balancing a mountain of student debt, endless exams, and life in general is no easy feat.

When I started looking for ways to earn extra income, I had no clue where to begin. My tech knowledge? Let's just say it wasn't exactly groundbreaking. But what I do have are medical research skills, and I decided to put them to work. I approached the world of side hustles, freelancing, and income streams the same way I would a complex medical problem: by researching thoroughly, testing ideas, and figuring out what works.

This book is the result of that process. It's packed with the strategies, tools, and tips I discovered—simple, actionable steps anyone can take to start earning more money. Whether you're a tech newbie like I was or someone just looking for a little guidance, there's something here for you.

One more thing: I have **no affiliations** with any of the platforms or tools mentioned in this book. I'm not getting paid to recommend them—they're just genuinely effective resources I've come across during my journey.

If I can figure this out while studying medicine and juggling life's chaos, I know you can too. Thanks for picking up this book, and let's get started on building your future today!

**Your fellow hustler,**
Galadriel

Quick Cash Playbook

## TABLE OF CONTENTS

Step-by-Step Srategies for Riding Today's Money-MakingTrends ....... i
About the Author ................................................... iii
**Introduction** ........................................................ 1
Chapter 1 ............................................................ 2
Why "Fast Money" Doesn't Mean "Easy Money" ...................... 2
**The 4 Growing Trends to Tap Into Right Now** ....................... 2
Chapter 2 ............................................................ 3
**What It Is** ......................................................... 3
   **Step-by-Step Plan** ............................................. 3
      **4. Monetize Your Content:** ................................. 4
      **Tools to Help You Succeed** ................................ 4
      Example ..................................................... 4
Chapter 3 ............................................................ 5
**What It Is** ......................................................... 5
**Step-by-Step Plan** ................................................. 5
Chapter 4 ............................................................ 7
**What It Is** ......................................................... 7
**Step-by-Step Plan** ................................................. 7
Chapter 5 ............................................................ 8
**What It Is** ......................................................... 8
**Step-by-Step Plan** ................................................. 8
**Conclusion: Take Action Today** .................................... 9
Chapter 6 ........................................................... 10
**1. Web3: The Decentralized Internet** ............................. 10
**Opportunities in Web3** ........................................... 10
**3. Play-to-Earn Games** ........................................... 11

How to Prepare for Web3 .................................................................. 11
Examples of Blockchain Gigs ........................................................... 12
Smart Contract Developers: ....................................................... 12

## 5. Data Validation and Staking .................................................. 12

## 6. Content Creation for DAOs (Decentralized Autonomous Organizations) ........................................................................ 13

## How to Prepare for Blockchain Gigs ......................................... 13

## How to Prepare for AI Opportunities ........................................ 13

Conclusion: Be Ready for What's Next ............................................ 14

## Chapter 7 ............................................................................................ 15

## Step 1: Sell Stuff You Already Own .......................................... 15

How to Start: ................................................................................. 15

Guaranteed Result: ....................................................................... 16

## Step 2: Do the Gig Hustle ........................................................... 16

What to Do: ................................................................................... 16

How to Make It Work: ................................................................. 16

Guaranteed Result: ....................................................................... 16

## Step 3: Offer Your Skills (Even If You Don't Think You Have Any) . 16

Guaranteed Result: ....................................................................... 17

## Step 4: Sell Your Voice (No, Not Like Ariel in The Little Mermaid) 17

How to Start: ................................................................................. 17

Guaranteed Result: ....................................................................... 18

How to Start: ................................................................................. 18

Guaranteed Result: ....................................................................... 18

## Step 6: The Side Hustle Surefire Combo Plan ....................... 18

Your Combo Plan: ........................................................................ 19

Final Word of Advice ................................................................... 19

## References and Resources ........................................................ 20

## Creator Economy Tools ............................................................. 20

**E-Commerce Platforms** ........................................................20
**Freelancing and Gig Work** ...................................................21
**AI Tools and Automation** ....................................................21
**Selling and Marketing Tools** ................................................21
**Investing Apps** ...............................................................22
**Learning Resources** ..........................................................22
**Bonus Tools** ..................................................................22

## INTRODUCTION

# WHY GETTING RICH TODAY IS EASIER THAN EVER

Making money isn't about luck or secret handshakes anymore. Thanks to technology and global trends, there are more ways than ever to earn fast cash and build wealth.

The good news? You don't need a degree, a fat bank account, or even a ton of free time. This book will break down the fastest, smartest ways to make money in today's world—step by step, trend by trend.

By the end, you'll have a roadmap to success, whether you want to pay off debt, save for something big, or finally quit your 9-to-5 job!

## CHAPTER 1
# THE FAST MONEY FORMULA

### WHY "FAST MONEY" DOESN'T MEAN "EASY MONEY"

Yes, you can make money quickly, but it still takes effort. The secret is to combine **speed** with **focus** by following these steps:

1. Find what's trending (we'll show you how).
2. Choose one idea to start with.
3. Follow the instructions in this book (we've got your back).

### THE 4 GROWING TRENDS TO TAP INTO RIGHT NOW

1. **The Creator Economy**: Making content for YouTube, TikTok, or Instagram.
2. **E-Commerce Boom**: Selling physical or digital products online.
3. **Freelancing and Gig Work**: Offering your skills or services.
4. **AI Tools and Automation**: Using tech to make tasks faster and easier.

## CHAPTER 2

# TREND #1 - THE CREATOR ECONOMY

## WHAT IT IS

The Creator Economy is about sharing videos, photos, or blogs that entertain, educate, or inspire—and getting paid for it. Think of YouTubers, TikTok creators, and Instagram influencers.

## STEP-BY-STEP PLAN

**1. PICK A PLATFORM:**

- **TikTok**: Great for short, funny, or educational videos.
- **YouTube**: Perfect for longer, in-depth content like tutorials or vlogs.
- **Instagram**: Best for photos, Reels, and inspirational posts.

**2. CHOOSE YOUR NICHE:**

What are you good at or passionate about? Examples:

- Cooking? Post recipes.
- DIY crafts? Show how it's done.
- Fitness? Share quick workout tips.

## 3. START POSTING (DON'T OVERTHINK IT):
Use these ideas:

- **TikTok**: Film a 15-second video showing "3 ways to use leftover pizza."
- **YouTube**: Post "5 beginner tips for knitting."
- **Instagram:** Share a motivational quote with a beautiful photo.

## 4. MONETIZE YOUR CONTENT:
Once you grow your audience, make money with:

- Sponsorships: Brands pay you to feature their products.
- Ads: YouTube pays you when people watch ads on your videos.
- Affiliate Links: Earn a cut when someone buys through your links.

## TOOLS TO HELP YOU SUCCEED

- **CapCut**: Free app to edit TikTok and Instagram videos.
- **Canva**: Create professional graphics and thumbnails.
- **TubeBuddy**: Optimize your YouTube videos for search.

## EXAMPLE

Lily, a high school teacher, started posting math tips on TikTok during her free time. Within six months, she had 100,000 followers and got a sponsorship deal from a tutoring app, earning $2,000 a month.

## CHAPTER 3

# Trend #2 - The E-Commerce Boom

### WHAT IT IS

E-commerce is just a fancy way of saying "selling stuff online." With platforms like Etsy, Shopify, and Amazon, you can set up a store in minutes and start selling.

### STEP-BY-STEP PLAN

1. **Decide What to Sell:**

   - **Handmade Goods:** Jewelry, candles, art (great for Etsy).

   - **Digital Products:** E-books, printables, or design templates (use Gumroad).

   - **Trending Products:** Buy and resell hot items like gadgets (try Amazon).

2. **Choose a Platform:**

   - **Etsy:** Perfect for handmade and creative products.

   - **Shopify:** Build your own store for total control.

   - **Amazon:** Sell almost anything to a massive audience.

3. **Create Your Store:**

   - Upload clear photos of your product.

   - Write a simple, catchy description (think "candles that smell like happiness").

## 4. Promote Your Products:

- Share photos and videos on TikTok or Instagram.
- Use hashtags like #HandmadeJewelry or #HomeDecor.

## 5. Get Reviews:

Ask your first customers to leave glowing reviews—it helps build trust.

### Example

Mike started making leather wallets as a hobby. He opened an Etsy shop and sold out his first batch within two weeks.

By month three, he was making $1,500 a month in extra income.

## CHAPTER 4
# TREND #3 - FREELANCING AND GIG WORK

### WHAT IT IS

Freelancing means getting paid to use your skills (like writing, designing, or tutoring). Gig work is about small tasks, like delivering food or assembling furniture.

### STEP-BY-STEP PLAN

**1. Pick a Platform:**

- **Fiverr:** Offer quick, affordable services.
- **Upwork:** Bid on bigger projects for higher pay.
- **TaskRabbit:** Get paid to run errands or fix things.

**2. Decide What to Offer:**

- Writing or proofreading.
- Designing logos or social media posts.
- Helping people move or clean their homes.

**3. Create a Profile:**

- Use a professional photo.
- Write a short description like: "I'll design a logo that makes your business stand out."

**4. Start Small, Then Raise Your Rates:**

- Take smaller jobs at first to get good reviews.
- Once you have reviews, charge more.

## CHAPTER 5

# TREND #4 - AI TOOLS AND AUTOMATION

### WHAT IT IS

AI (Artificial Intelligence) tools can save you time and help you make money faster by automating tasks like writing, designing, or customer service.

### STEP-BY-STEP PLAN

1. **Use AI for Side Hustles**:

   - **Writing**: Use ChatGPT to help write blog posts or e-books.
   - **Design**: Use Canva with AI-generated templates.
   - **Customer Service**: Use tools like Zendesk for handling messages.

2. **Sell AI Services**:

   - Offer "AI-powered" content creation to small businesses.
   - Use AI to design logos or social media posts.

3. **Combine AI with E-commerce**:

   - Create digital products like printable calendars using AI design tools.
   - Use AI to analyze trends and find winning products.

**Example**

Chris used ChatGPT to create a 20-page e-book about healthy meal prep. He sold it for $10 on Gumroad, earning $500 in his first month.

## CONCLUSION: TAKE ACTION TODAY

Success isn't about waiting for the perfect moment—it's about starting now. Pick one trend, follow the steps, and take your first action today.

Whether it's posting your first TikTok, opening an Etsy shop, or offering a gig on Fiverr, every small step adds up.

## CHAPTER 6

# DEEP DIVE ON FUTURE TRENDS – STAYING AHEAD OF THE GAME

The world is changing fast, and new opportunities to make money are popping up everywhere. The key to staying ahead isn't about luck—it's about being ready for the next big thing.

This chapter will explore three **emerging trends** that are shaping the future of work and wealth creation: **Web3, blockchain-based gigs, and AI advancements.**

### 1. WEB3: THE DECENTRALIZED INTERNET

**What Is Web3?**

Web3 is the next generation of the internet, where control shifts from big corporations to individuals. It's powered by technologies like blockchain, which makes transactions secure and transparent. Imagine owning your digital content or getting paid directly for your data—Web3 is making that possible.

### OPPORTUNITIES IN WEB3

**1. NFTs (Non-Fungible Tokens)**

**What They Are**: Digital assets like art, music, or collectibles that can be bought, sold, or traded.

**How to Get Started**:

- Create unique digital content (art, music, e-books) and sell it as NFTs on platforms like **OpenSea** or **Rarible**.

- Example, an Artist sold a simple drawing for $10,000 as an NFT.

## 2. Decentralized Finance (DeFi)

**What It Is**: A system where you can earn interest, trade, or borrow without banks.

**How to Get Started**:

- Use platforms like **Aave** or **Compound** to earn interest on your crypto investments.

- Example: Some users earn 10–15% annual returns on their savings through DeFi.

## 3. PLAY-TO-EARN GAMES

**What They Are**: Video games where players earn cryptocurrency or digital assets by playing.

**How to Get Started**:

- Join popular games like **Axie Infinity** or **Decentraland**.

- Example: Players in some countries earn a full-time income from these games.

### HOW TO PREPARE FOR WEB3

**Learn the Basics**:

- Take free courses on platforms like Coursera or YouTube.

- Join communities like **r/Web3** on Reddit to stay updated.

**Experiment:**

- Buy a small amount of cryptocurrency and explore how wallets and NFTs work.

- Use free tools like **MetaMask** to set up a crypto wallet.

## 4. Blockchain-Based Gigs

### What Are Blockchain-Based Gigs?
These are jobs or tasks powered by blockchain platforms, where payments are secure, transparent, and often in cryptocurrency. Think of it as freelancing 2.0.

**EXAMPLES OF BLOCKCHAIN GIGS**

### SMART CONTRACT DEVELOPERS:

**What They Do:** Write programs that automatically execute agreements when conditions are met.

- **Earning Potential:** $60–$200/hour.

- **How to Start:** Learn programming languages like Solidity (used for Ethereum).

## 5. DATA VALIDATION AND STAKING

**What It Is:** Validate transactions or stake cryptocurrency to support blockchain networks and earn rewards.

- **How to Start:** Use platforms like **Cardano** or **Polkadot**.

## 6. CONTENT CREATION FOR DAOS (DECENTRALIZED AUTONOMOUS ORGANIZATIONS)

**What It Is**: DAOs are groups that make decisions collectively using blockchain. They often hire content creators, marketers, or developers.

- **How to Start**: Join DAOs like **Friends with Benefits** or **Mirror.xyz** and offer your skills.

## HOW TO PREPARE FOR BLOCKCHAIN GIGS

**Learn Blockchain Basics**:

1) Platforms like CryptoZombies offer gamified tutorials for learning coding on the blockchain.

2) **Build Your Portfolio**: Offer small blockchain-related tasks on platforms like **Gitcoin** to gain experience.

## HOW TO PREPARE FOR AI OPPORTUNITIES

**Experiment with AI Tools**:

1) Try free versions of tools like **Jasper, DALL·E,** or **RunwayML. Upskill with Free Resources**: Pllatforms like Google AI and Udemy offer beginner-friendly courses.

## CONCLUSION: BE READY FOR WHAT'S NEXT

The future is full of opportunities—you just need to take the first step. Whether you're diving into Web3, exploring blockchain gigs, or leveraging AI tools, the key is to keep learning and experimenting.

By staying curious and adaptable, you'll be ready to ride the next wave of trends—and maybe even get rich doing it!

## CHAPTER 7

# STILL LOST? LET'S GUARANTEE THAT INCOME

Okay, so you've read the strategies, skimmed the examples (it's okay, we're all guilty of it), and you're still sitting there thinking, *"Yeah, but what do I actually DO?"*

Don't worry—I've got you covered. Let's break it down even simpler. You're here for guaranteed results, so I'll give you foolproof steps to start earning, even if you have no clue where to begin.

### STEP 1: SELL STUFF YOU ALREADY OWN

Yes, it's the old "clean out your closet" trick, but hear me out. People will pay good money for things collecting dust in your house.

**HOW TO START:**

1. **Find It**: Look for clothes, gadgets, books, or furniture you don't use anymore.

2. **List It**: Post on **Facebook Marketplace**, **eBay**, or **Poshmark**. Use these magic words in your description:

    - "Gently used" (even if it's been in your garage since the Bush administration).
    - "Priced to sell fast."

3. **Sell It**: Set a reasonable price and respond quickly to buyers.

**GUARANTEED RESULT:**

You'll have cash in hand within days—and less clutter to boot. Win-win.

## STEP 2: DO THE GIG HUSTLE

If you've got a car, a bike, or just some free time, you can get paid to help people out.

**WHAT TO DO:**

- Sign up for **DoorDash**, **Uber Eats**, or **TaskRabbit**.

- Deliver food, assemble furniture, or run errands for folks who can't (or won't) do it themselves.

**HOW TO MAKE IT WORK:**

- Work during peak hours (lunch/dinner for food delivery).

- Pick gigs that fit your skills. If you've never held a hammer, maybe skip the furniture assembly.

**GUARANTEED RESULT:**

Gigs like this pay fast—sometimes same-day. You could easily make $100–$200 in a weekend.

## STEP 3: OFFER YOUR SKILLS (EVEN IF YOU DON'T THINK YOU HAVE ANY)

Trust me, everyone's good at something, and someone out there is willing to pay for it.

**How to Start:**

1. **Think Small**: Can you type? Proofread? Draw a decent stick figure? Start there.

2. **Pick a Platform**:
   - **Fiverr** for small tasks like writing or design.
   - **Upwork** for larger freelance projects.

3. **Create a Simple Offer**:
   - Example: "I'll write a 500-word blog post for $30."
   - Bonus: Add a "fast delivery" option for an extra $10.

**GUARANTEED RESULT:**

Even basic skills can earn you $200–$500 a month once you start landing gigs.

## STEP 4: SELL YOUR VOICE (NO, NOT LIKE ARIEL IN THE LITTLE MERMAID)

AI tools have made it easier than ever to sell audio content—even if you're not a professional voice actor.

**HOW TO START:**

1. Use **Murf AI** or **Resemble AI** to generate professional-quality voiceovers.

2. Offer services on Fiverr or Upwork for podcast intros, YouTube videos, or audiobooks.

**GUARANTEED RESULT:**

You can charge $50–$300 per project, and no one even has to hear your real voice.

## Step 5: Resell Popular Items (No, You Don't Need a Warehouse)

Buy low, sell high. It's as simple as that.

**HOW TO START:**

1. Look for deals at thrift stores, clearance sales, or Facebook Marketplace.

2. Flip those items on platforms like eBay or Poshmark.

3. Focus on hot items like brand-name shoes, gadgets, or collectibles.

**GUARANTEED RESULT:**

Flipping items can easily bring in $500–$1,000 a month if you're consistent.

## STEP 6: THE SIDE HUSTLE SUREFIRE COMBO PLAN

Still unsure which path to take? Let's do a combo for guaranteed results.

## YOUR COMBO PLAN:

1. **Day 1–5**: Sell 10 items you already own.

2. **Day 6–10**: Sign up for DoorDash or Uber Eats and complete your first gig.

3. **Day 11–15**: Create a simple Fiverr gig offering a skill (even if it's proofreading memes).

4. **Day 16–30**: Take the money you've earned so far and invest in items to resell.

---

## FINAL WORD OF ADVICE

If you're sitting there thinking, *"I don't know where to start"*, just pick one thing from this list and do it today.

Not tomorrow. Not "after I research some more." Today. Guaranteed income isn't about magic; it's about action. So get out there and start earning!

# REFERENCES

## REFERENCES AND RESOURCES

Here's a list of all the tools, platforms, and resources mentioned in this book, conveniently linked for quick access. These are tried-and-true tools to help you take action right away.

## CREATOR ECONOMY TOOLS

1. TikTok - Platform for creating short, engaging videos.
2. YouTube - The go-to platform for long-form video content.
3. Instagram - Ideal for photos, Reels, and building a visual brand.
4. CapCut - Free and easy video editing app for TikTok and Instagram content.
5. Canva - Design tool for thumbnails, social media posts, and more.
6. TubeBuddy - YouTube optimization tool to boost your videos' visibility.

## E-COMMERCE PLATFORMS

7. Etsy - Marketplace for handmade and creative products.
8. Shopify - Build your own online store with full customization.
9. Amazon Seller Central - Start selling on Amazon's massive platform.
10. Gumroad - Sell digital products like e-books or printables.

## FREELANCING AND GIG WORK

11. Fiverr - Offer quick and affordable freelance services.
12. Upwork - Bid on high-value freelance projects.
13. TaskRabbit - Get paid for helping with errands and small tasks.

## AI TOOLS AND AUTOMATION

14. ChatGPT - AI tool for writing, brainstorming, and content creation.
15. Canva AI - AI-powered design templates for professional graphics.
16. Zendesk - Customer service tool for handling messages and queries.

## SELLING AND MARKETING TOOLS

17. Facebook Marketplace - Sell items locally and connect with buyers.
18. eBay - Great for selling gadgets, collectibles, and used items.
19. Poshmark - Perfect for selling clothes and accessories.

## INVESTING APPS

20. Robinhood - Easy stock trading app for beginners.
21. Acorns - Automatically invest spare change.
22. Fundrise - Invest in real estate with as little as $10.

## LEARNING RESOURCES

23. YouTube Creator Academy - Learn how to grow your YouTube channel.
24. HubSpot Blog - Free guides on digital marketing and business growth.
25. **Neil Patel Blog** - Marketing tips and SEO insights for beginners.

## BONUS TOOLS

26. Zapier - Automate repetitive tasks to save time.
27. QuickBooks - Manage your finances and invoices effortlessly.
28. Skillshare - Affordable courses on everything from video editing to marketing.

www.ingramcontent.com/pod-product-compliance
Lightning Source LLC
Chambersburg PA
CBHW070945220526
45469CB00007B/2525

## ABOUT THIS BOOK

Unlock the secrets to financial success with "Quick Cash Playbook"! Dive into today's to money-making trends with this no-nonsense guide.

Whether you're exploring side hustles, freelancing, the latest in digital finance, this book offer straightforward, step-by-step strategies that anyon can follow. Inside, you'll discover how to: Choos profitable side hustles that fit your lifestyle. Maste the gig economy and maximize your earnings. Inves smartly in cryptocurrencies and digital assets.

Leverage social media for business gains. Develo passive income streams for long-term benefit "Quick Cash Playbook" equips you with the tools yo need to increase your income effectively, blendin expert advice with practical steps and real-worl examples.

Transform your financial future today!